## Advance Praise for
## *Nuts in Nutland*

A poet versed in rhyme and meter
creates a book that charmed this reader!
—**Lesléa Newman** author of *Heather Has Two Mommies*

Mary Meriam's *Nuts in Nutland,* delightfully illustrated by Hannah Barrett, is a joyful poetic adventure through an imagined domain populated by nuts and the occasional legume. Offering a message that emphasizes the importance of accepting differences and versed in playful rhymed couplets, *Nuts in Nutland* uses language and imagery both inviting and educational for a young reader. Presenting a simple story in a dynamic and rhythmical manner, and with colorful, fun illustrations accompanying the poem, *Nuts in Nutland* is an entertaining new entry in the long tradition of poetry for children, reminiscent at moments of the verses to be found in Lewis Carroll's *Alice in Wonderland* or of T.S. Eliot's *Old Possum's Book of Practical Cats* in its wit and charm.
—**Stu Watson** editor of *Prelude*

*Nuts in Nutland* joyfully reminds us that we are all connected. That love, earth, and sustenance grow in tandem whether we recognize it or not.
—**Angela Dufresne** artist

Text © 2018 by Mary Meriam. All rights reserved.
Illustrations © 2018 by Hannah Barrett. All rights reserved.

ISBN-13: 978-0999593011
ISBN-10: 0999593013

This book may not be reproduced, in whole or in part, including illustrations, in any form (beyond that permitted by Sections 107 and 108 of the U.S. Copyright Law and except by reviewers for the public press), without written permission from the publishers.

ACKNOWLEDGMENTS

Mary Meriam thanks:
Robert Schechter for this poem's prompt.
Kate Wolford for selecting this poem as the winner of the January, 2013, *Enchanted Conversations* contest.
Lillian Faderman for being my muse.

Hannah Barrett thanks:
Laurel Sparks for her encouragement and support of the project and Jack and Ellen Barrett for their love of books and reading.

PUBLISHER

Headmistress Press / Sally Jane Books
60 Shipview Lane
Sequim, WA 98382
Telephone: 917-428-8312
Email: sallyjanebooks@gmail.com
Website: headmistresspress.blogspot.com

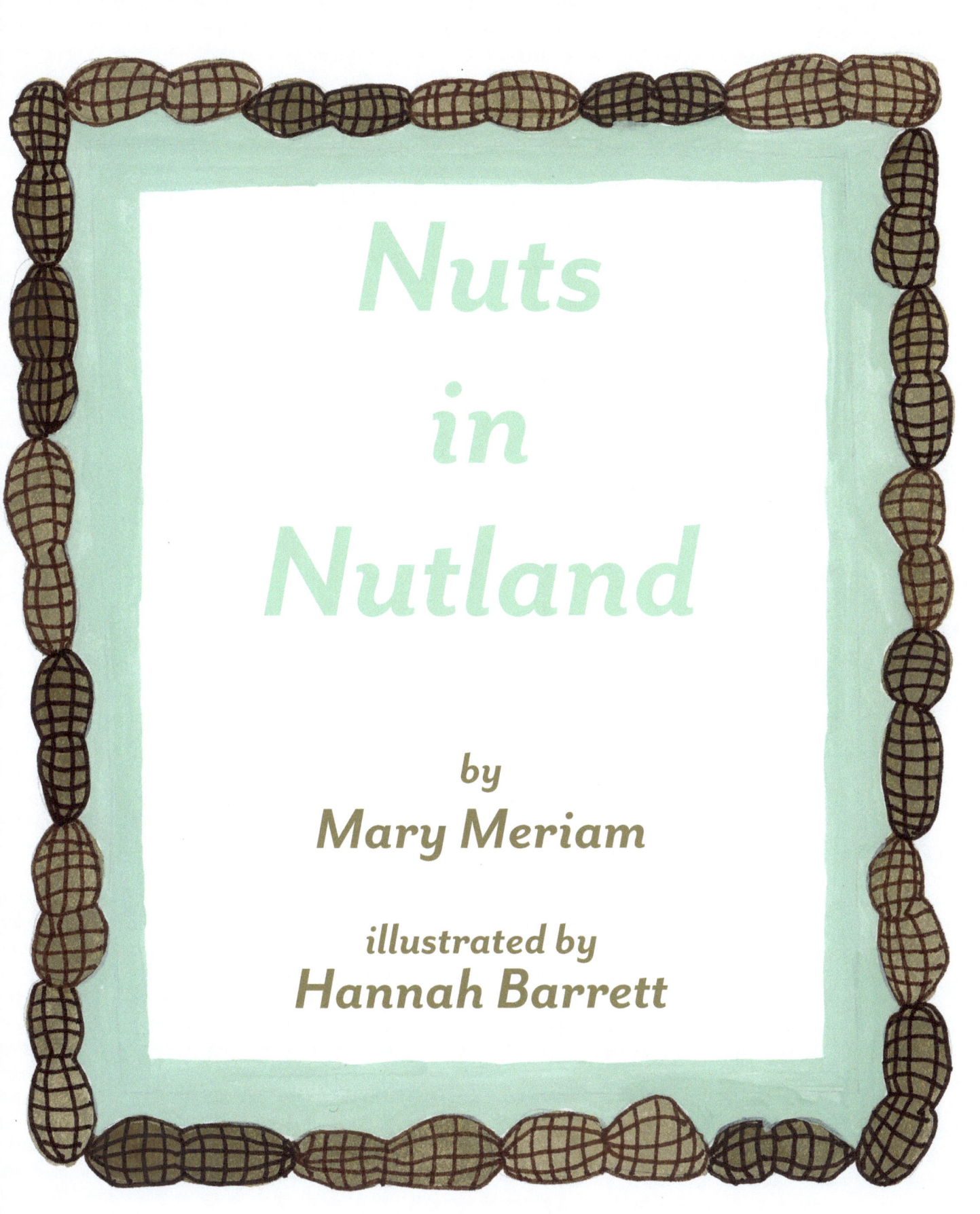

# Nuts in Nutland

by
**Mary Meriam**

illustrated by
**Hannah Barrett**

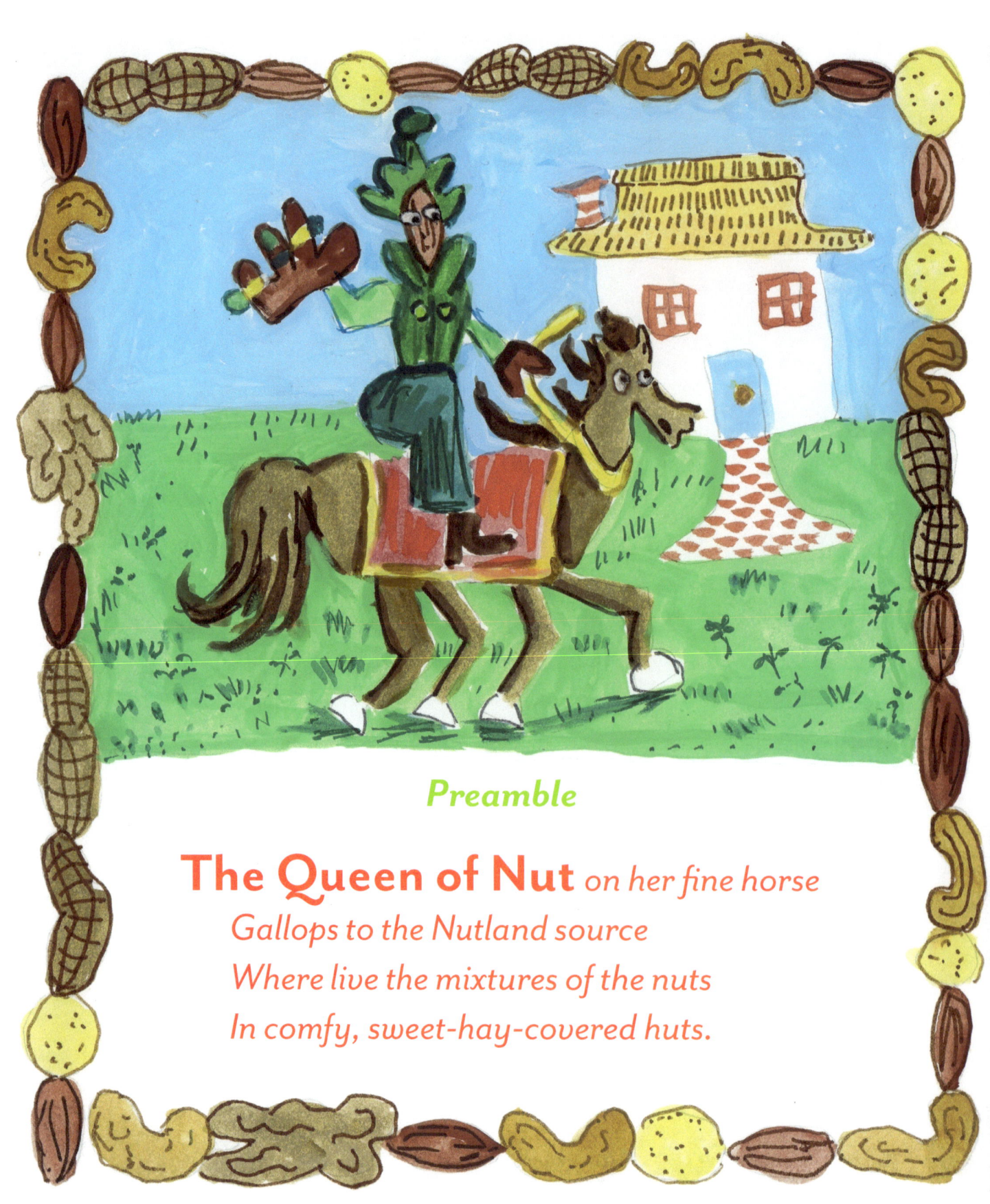

### *Preamble*

**The Queen of Nut** on her fine horse
Gallops to the Nutland source
Where live the mixtures of the nuts
In comfy, sweet-hay-covered huts.

**"Hallo!"** she cries, to wake the dead,
But wakes a maiden up instead
Who drops her heavy pot of soup
And runs out past the chicken coop
To see the Queen of Nut ride by.

Alas, this makes the **Cashew** cry
And fills **Pecan** with woe and grief.
The nuts all weep in disbelief.
The **Queen of Nut** is kindly, and
She wishes she could understand
How nuts of Nutland all are feeling.
Maybe she can do some healing.

### *Invocation*

"**O Goddess Nut of Egypt,** show
The nuts of Nutland here below
Thy wisdom and thy goddess powers,
Bring them happiness and flowers."

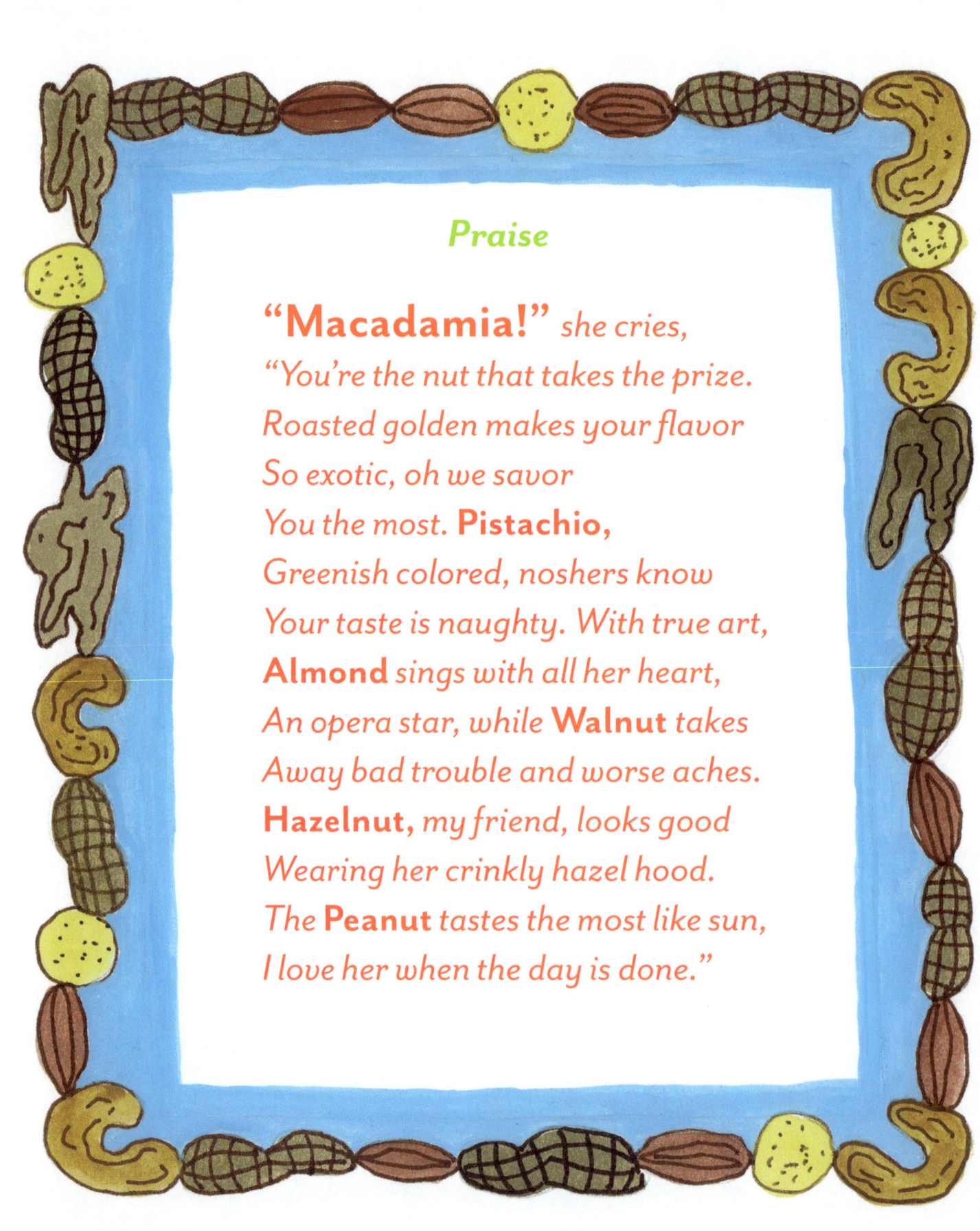

### Praise

**"Macadamia!"** she cries,
"You're the nut that takes the prize.
Roasted golden makes your flavor
So exotic, oh we savor
You the most. **Pistachio,**
Greenish colored, noshers know
Your taste is naughty. With true art,
**Almond** sings with all her heart,
An opera star, while **Walnut** takes
Away bad trouble and worse aches.
**Hazelnut,** my friend, looks good
Wearing her crinkly hazel hood.
The **Peanut** tastes the most like sun,
I love her when the day is done."

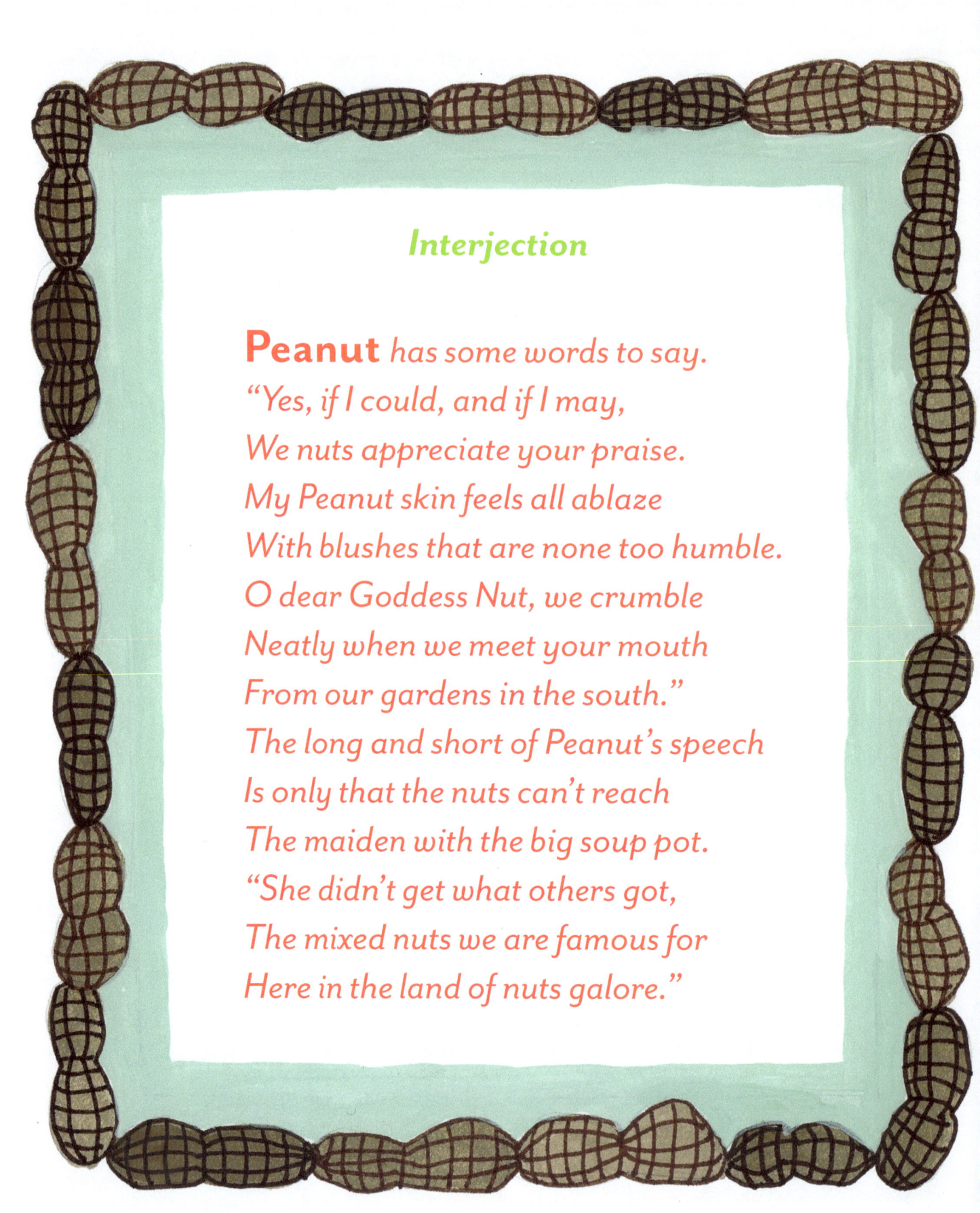

### Interjection

**Peanut** has some words to say.
"Yes, if I could, and if I may,
We nuts appreciate your praise.
My Peanut skin feels all ablaze
With blushes that are none too humble.
O dear Goddess Nut, we crumble
Neatly when we meet your mouth
From our gardens in the south."
The long and short of Peanut's speech
Is only that the nuts can't reach
The maiden with the big soup pot.
"She didn't get what others got,
The mixed nuts we are famous for
Here in the land of nuts galore."

### Suggestion

**The Queen of Nut**, who's listening,
Each ring of emerald glistening,
Suggests to Goddess Nut, "Perhaps
America will not collapse,
Not to mention Nutland too,
If this maiden with the stew…"
(Here Peanut interrupts to say,
"Not stew, it's soup.") "Okay, okay,"
The Queen continues, "with the soup,
Were to receive a whole nut group,
A mixed-nut package, as it were,
Whatever nuts she might prefer.
We, the Queen of Nut, now wish
To meet the maiden with the dish."

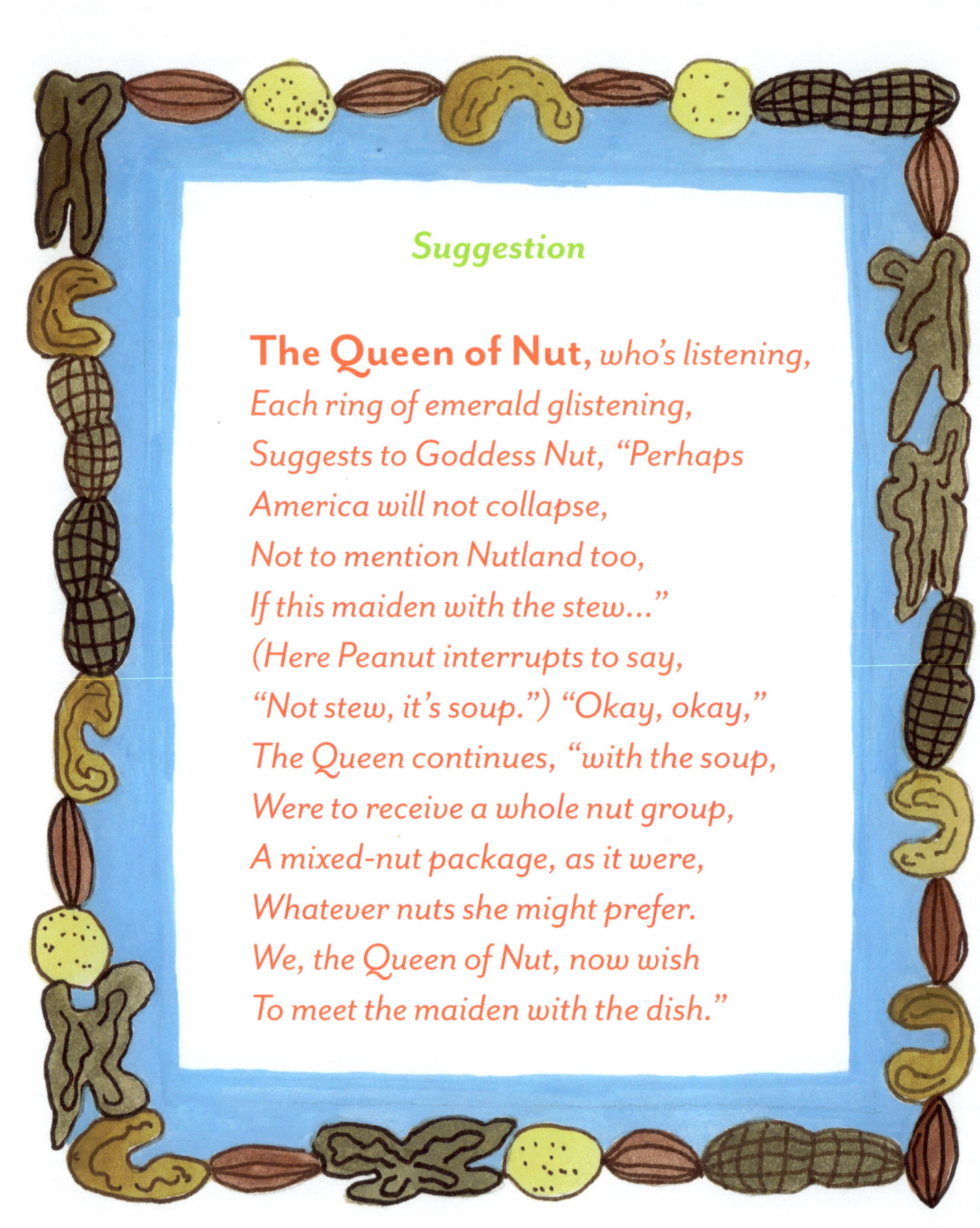

### Magic

The **Goddess** beams from up above
And sows some seeds of goddess love.
Meanwhile, **Maiden Soup** sits weeping,
Spilled soup all around her seeping,
Nothing left for her to eat.
Plop-plop her tears fall on her feet

And also on the arid earth
That always seemed of little worth.
But now, amazingly, but true,
Flowers of lemon, rose, and blue
Appear like magic, oh so fair.
She puts the flowers in her hair.

**Then the Goddess** *swallows whole*
*The sun, so evening can unroll*

Her indigo and starry cloth
And trade the butterfly for moth.

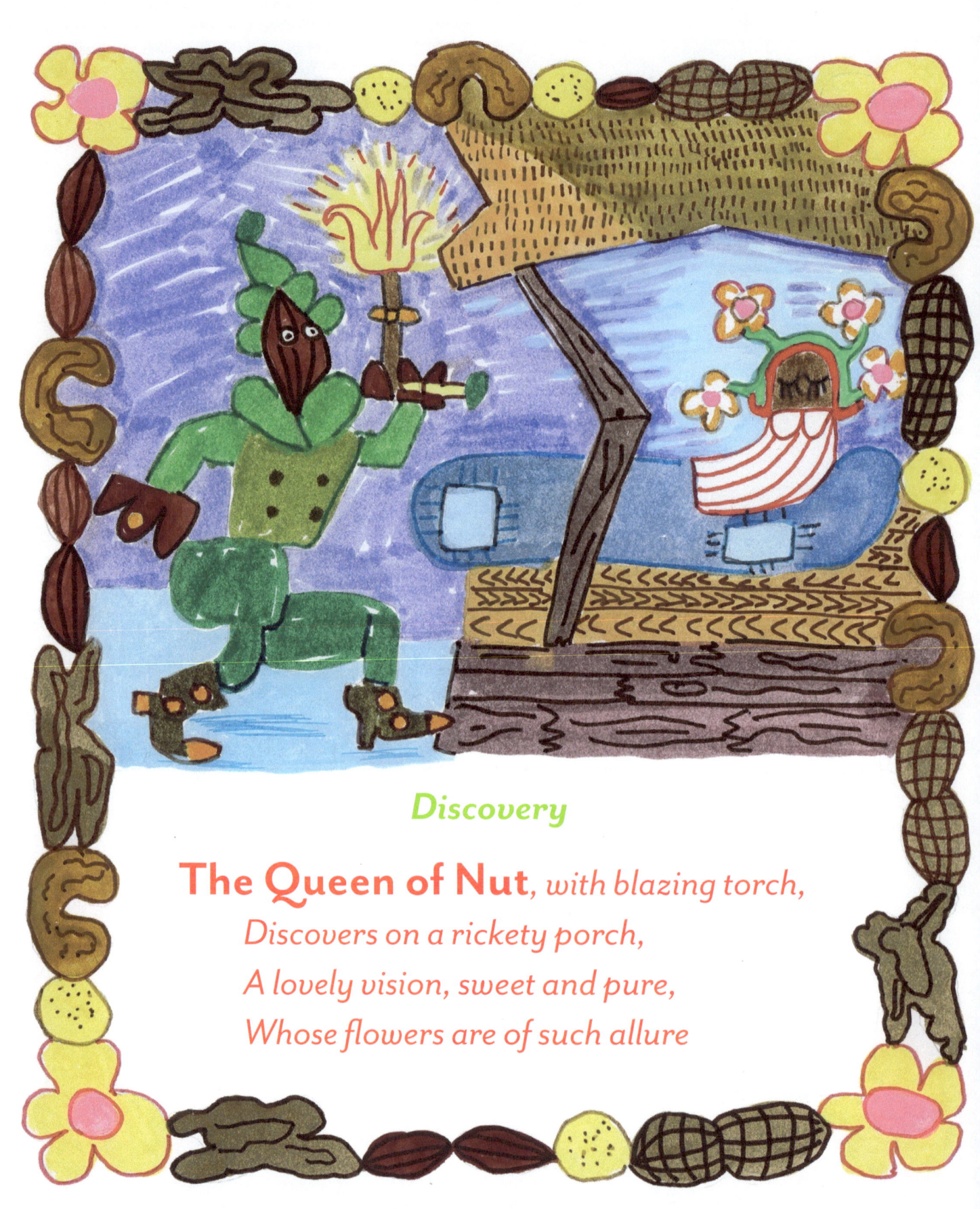

### *Discovery*

**The Queen of Nut**, *with blazing torch,*
*Discovers on a rickety porch,*
*A lovely vision, sweet and pure,*
*Whose flowers are of such allure*

She kneels at once and lifts her up
And offers her her loving cup
(Along with endless roasted nuts).
To test the truth, the maiden shuts
Her violet eyes then opens them,
A blossom blooming on its stem.

### Denoument

**The Goddess Nut** gives birth to sun,
Another Nutland day begun,
And Maiden Soup looks fresh and new,
As if the daylight loves her too.

*With pounding hearts and horse's hoofs*
*The lovers ride toward Nutland's roofs*
*With plans to marry, and to meet*
*The nuts they love so much to eat.*

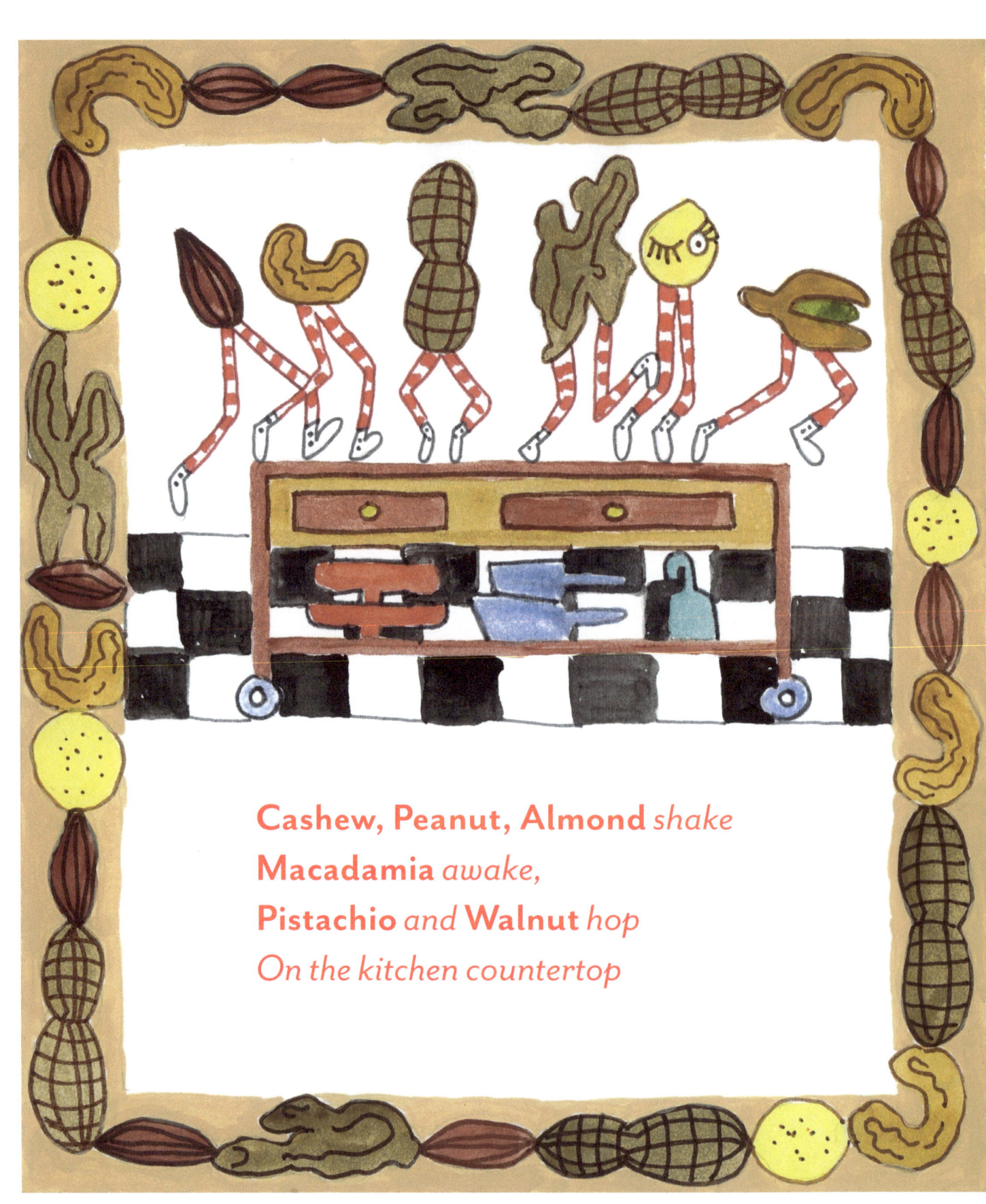

**Cashew, Peanut, Almond** *shake*
**Macadamia** *awake,*
**Pistachio** *and* **Walnut** *hop*
*On the kitchen countertop*

With **Hazelnut**, and mix and roast
And raise their nutshells for a toast:
Long live **Nutland Queen** and **Maiden**
With our tables fully laden!

**Farewell from all the Nuts in Nutland**

www.ingramcontent.com/pod-product-compliance
Lightning Source LLC
Chambersburg PA
CBHW041958150426
43193CB00003B/52